Alessandro Cecchi

AGNOLO
BRONZINO

SCALA

INDEX

Photographic acknowledgements: SCALA ARCHIVE
except for nos. 1, 61, 62 (reproduced by courtesy of the Trustees,
The National Gallery, London); no. 7 (Pinacoteca del Castello
Sforzesco, Milan/M. Saporetti); nos. 16, 17, 27 (Artothek Spezialarchiv
für Gemäldefotografien, Peissenberg); no. 20 (© Board of Trustees,
National Gallery of Art, Washington); nos. 24, 26 (© Bildarchiv
Preussischer Kulturbesitz, Berlin); nos. 41, 42, 43, 45 (Besançon,
Musée des Beaux-Arts et d'Archéologie, Cliché Charles Choffet);
no. 66 (Copyright The Frick Collection, New York); no. 73 (P. Tosi,
Florence); no. 74 (Izobrazitelnoye Iskusstvo)
Translation: Christopher Evans
Editing: Marilena Vecchi
Printed in Italy by: Arti Grafiche "Stampa Nazionale",
Calenzano (Florence), 1996

1. Pontormo
*Joseph in Egypt, detail, portrait of Bronzino
as a youth (on the left)
London, National Gallery*

His Origins and Apprenticeship with Pontormo (1503-1530)

Agnolo di Cosimo di Mariano was born on November 17, 1503, in the heavily populated suburb of Monticelli, outside the Porta a San Frediano on the road to Pisa. He was the son of a butcher and a woman called Felice about whom we know nothing further. Probably as a result of the boy's own inclinations, his parents soon apprenticed him to a mediocre painter and then to Raffaellino del Garbo to learn the "principles of art" (Vasari).

However the young man, better known by his pseudonym of Bronzino, was not to make greater strides until he came under the skilled guidance of Jacopo Carrucci called Pontormo (1494-1557). Although Pontormo was "extremely rough and strange" even with the disciples he most appreciated, "such was Agnolo's patience and affection toward [his master], that he was forced to grow fond of him and love him like a son," initiating an association that was to last for the whole of Pontormo's life.

Evidence for this comes from the fact that they continued to collaborate at least until 1537, when Bronzino was already an independent artist, and from the frequent dinners and lunches with his former pupil recorded in the *Diary* that Carrucci kept from 1554 to 1556. Another touching sign of this affectionate relationship can be found in the portrait of Agnolo that Pontormo inserted into one of his *Scenes from the Life of Joseph the Patriarch* for the wooden decoration of the nuptial chamber of Pierfrancesco Borgherini and Margherita Acciaiuoli, painted in collaboration with Andrea del Sarto, Granacci, and Bachiacca. At the foot of the staircase on which Joseph presents his father Jacob to the Pharaoh, in the compartment now in the National Gallery in London, the young man is depicted with a broad face framed with red hair, turned toward a devil-may-care youth with an equally red shock of hair, and appears – this was presum-

3

2, 3, 6. Bronzino
The Evangelists Matthew and Mark
diam. 70 cm each
Florence, Santa Felicita

4, 5. Pontormo
The Evangelists John and Luke
Florence, Santa Felicita

ably in the winter of 1517 or 1518, the date generally assigned to the painting – to have just returned from his daily chores or about to set off on an errand for the workshop, with his hat, short cloak, and a large basket in his right hand.

When the plague, which had broken out in Rome in the fall of 1522 and soon spread to Florence, in spite of the measures taken to prevent it, at the beginning of November of the same year, began to claim its first victims, Pontormo decided to seek safety from the terrible scourge by accepting the commission to decorate the cloister of the Carthusian monastery of San Lorenzo at Galluzzo, "taking with him only Bronzino; and having tasted that way of life, the quiet, the silence, and the solitude (all things in accord with Jacopo's inclinations and nature), he thought he would use the occasion to let his paintings reveal great strength of effort, and to show the world that they had come to express greater perfection and a different manner of style from the works he had done previously" (Vasari). And while the master attended to the frescoes in the cloister, painting *Scenes from the Passion* with angular and elongated figures, in the "German manner" and drawing on prints by Dürer, that are now ruined by exposure to the elements, the young Agnolo was given the job of decorating two lunettes with a *Dead Christ and Two Angels* and a *Martyrdom of Saint Lawrence* above the door leading from the main cloister into the chapter house. It is not possible to judge the quality of these paintings owing to their poor state of preservation, but it is likely that they were very modest efforts, a long way from the excellence that Bronzino was to demonstrate later.

Even though the plague was over by March 22, 1523, Pontormo remained at the Charterhouse for another two years, won over by monastic life. Toward the end of this period, in 1525, he painted the revolutionary *Supper at Emmaus* now in the Uffizi, while Agnolo, as well as assisting him in his normal functions as an apprentice, illuminated some of the Carthusian friars' liturgical books, now lost, and painted a *Crucifix* that remained in the master's possession and was later sold, according to Vasari, as his own work.

By the age of twenty-two Bronzino seems to have been enrolled in the Compagnia di San Luca, or guild of painters, and it was in that same year of 1525 that he must have received his first independent commission from the "black" Benedictine monks of the Badia Fiorentina, for whom he frescoed a large lunette with a picture of *Saint Benedict Repentant and in Ecstasy*, formerly in the Chiostro degli Aranci and now detached and transferred onto canvas. While this displays a strict adherence to the figurative modules of Jacopo, it is also characterized by a gentler and more melancholic vein and an attention to the landscape that softens the painting's tormented and visionary atmosphere.

This different feeling, barely detectable and certainly attenuated by the fact that Bronzino was painting to designs by Carrucci, can be found in some of the *Evangelists* in the tondi on the ceiling of the Capponi Chapel in Santa Felicita, probably painted around 1525, at the be-ginning of the work on which Pontormo and Bronzino would be engaged until 1528. As Vasari only attributes two of the tondi to Bronzino, without specifying which, scholars are still divided over which and how many of them were painted by the apprentice. In our opinion he was responsible for the *Saint Matthew* with an intense gaze, half-closed mouth, and tousled red hair, painted with thickly laid-on and glowing brushstrokes and enlivened by the strong light that falls on the figure with a swirling crimson cloak, set against the dark background, and for the *Saint Mark* with its palette of yellow and red tones contrasting with the green of the mantle wrapped around the figure, which looks as if it is peering through a window, an idea drawn from the Gospel. Perhaps the *Saint Luke* should also be considered a contribution by Agnolo to the decoration of the chapel, while the bald *Saint John* with a long beard seems to share the same uneasy and sorrowful humanity lavished on the body of Christ in the *Deposition* by Pontormo in the same chapel. This is almost evanescent in its pale and sharp colors, caught in what appears to be the dazzling glare of limelight, like the *Angel* and the *Annunciation* on the outer wall, at the sides of the window. The *Saint Sebastian* in the Thyssen-Bornemisza collection in Madrid, to which attention has been drawn by Cox Rearick, with a composition and style similar to the *Evangelists* of Santa Felicita, should also be assigned to this period.

In those years Pontormo also painted a tondo of the *Madonna and Child* for the Capponi, which is still in their palace in Florence, and Bronzino the *Holy Family with Saint Elizabeth and the Young Saint John* now in the National Gallery in Washington, assigned to him by Smyth. A preparatory drawing for the latter, representing only St Elizabeth, is in the Gabinetto Disegni e Stampe of the Uffizi (no. 6552 F recto).

While it seems possible to detect the first, timid signs of Agnolo breaking away from the style of Pontormo in the picture in the American collection, in his *Portrait of a Young Man* in the Civiche Raccolte of the Castello Sforzesco in Milan, the master's influence is still so strong that for forty years critics were led to believe, without a shadow of doubt, that it was by Jacopo. In fact the portrait can be identified as that of "Lorenzo Lenzi, now [in 1568] Bishop of Fermo," recorded by Vasari among those painted by Bronzino, as is clear from the sonnet "Famose Fronde de cui santi honori..." transcribed on one of the two pages of the book he is holding in his right hand and dedicated by Benedetto Varchi to Lenzi. The two had met in the summer of 1527 at Bivigliano, where the young man, together with his family and his tutor Annibal Caro, had taken refuge from the plague in the villa of Ugo della Stufa. It is likely that Bronzino, a great friend of Varchi's and more or less the same age, had also found sanctuary in this place during an enforced interruption in the work on the Capponi Chapel in Santa Felicita, which may have lasted from June 2, 1527, to the end of 1528, so serious was this fresh outbreak of the disease in Florence.

In his elegant garment of gray cloth with blue sleeves and trimmings, tied with ribbons fixed with golden pins,

7. Portrait of Lorenzo Lenzi
98x73 cm
Milan, Civiche Raccolte del Castello Sforzesco

8, 9. Pietà
115x100 cm
Florence, Uffizi

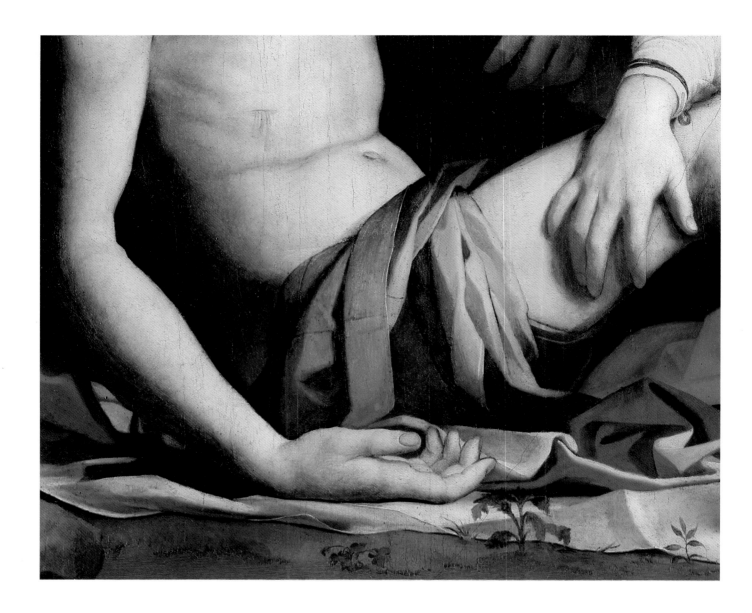

10. Pietà, detail
Florence, Uffizi

11. Drawing for a 'Noli me tangere'
385x281 mm
Florence, Uffizi, Gabinetto Disegni e Stampe,
no. 6633 F

the young Lorenzo (Florence 1516-?) stares at us, caught as if in a snapshot with his eyes wide open, apparently dazzled by the bright light that falls on his face, with the chubby cheeks of an adolescent, set against a green background. The portrait, in a mellow and elegant version of Pontormo's style and presumably dating, for the reasons outlined above, from the beginning of 1528, is therefore the earliest one by Bronzino that we know of. It was the first in a long series that, as we shall see, earned him much of his reputation. Among them was a small portrait, now lost, of Annibal Caro, painted prior to the latter's departure for Rome in 1529, in the capacity of secretary to Monsignor Gaddi.

It is to these years, as Smyth had proposed on the basis of its style and as has recently been confirmed by documents unearthed by Waldmann, that we should assign the *Pietà* in the Uffizi. This can be considered the same picture as the one in Santa Trinita that Vasari states was painted prior to the siege of Florence, even though it does not depict St John the Evangelist, perhaps because the panel has been cut down. In this painting Bronzino shows that he has shaken off the direct influence of his

10

*12. Pontormo
The Ten Thousand
Martyrs
65x73 cm
Florence
Galleria Palatina*

teacher's style, while retaining and accentuating its "pathos." This can plainly be seen in the panel in the Uffizi, where all the tragedy is contained in the sorrowful gazes of the Virgin and the Magdalen, both turned on the lifeless body of Christ, who appears to be smiling at his imminent triumph over death. There appears to be a link between the *Pietà* and two preparatory drawings for the lost *Noli me tangere* in the convent of the Franciscan "Poverine," one for the entire composition in a private collection and another for Christ's drapery alone, drawn in red pencil, in the Gabinetto Disegni e Stampe of the Uffizi.

Shortly afterward, Pontormo and Bronzino were to be caught up in new and dramatic events when the Florentine republic, reestablished in the spring of 1527 following the sack of Rome and the departure of the Medici, found itself fighting for survival, with the city under siege from imperial troops led by the Prince of Orange. According to Vasari, it was at this time that Pontormo painted *The Ten Thousand Martyrs* "for the women of the Hospital of the Innocenti," which is unanimously identified with the small picture in the Galleria Palatina. For Carlo Neroni, a Florentine of fierce republican beliefs, he painted a similar picture "but with only the battle scene of the martyrs, and the angel who is baptizing

them." This can be identified with the small panel in the Galleria degli Uffizi, in which Pontormo drew on the assistance of Bronzino, as is revealed by the noticeable differences in style between the two works, pointed out by scholars who have at the same time drawn attention to the fact that the drawings for both paintings were done by Pontormo. In the "reduced" version in the Uffizi, Bronzino appears to have used Pontormo's drawings for the Pitti *Martyrdom* in a different way, varying the composition by moving around whole groups of figures, eliminating some of them and adding new ones in the foreground on the left. The figures themselves, moreover, are hardly more than sketched in thickly laid-on paint, unlike those of Pontormo, which are defined by subtle and incisive drawing and light and luminous tints.

During the siege, which was brought to an end by the city's surrender in the August of 1530, and at a time when the streets resounded with the explosions of bombards and the clamor of fighting, Carrucci portrayed not only Neroni, but also "Francesco Guardi in the garb of a soldier, which was a very fine work; and afterward on the cover of this picture, Bronzino painted Pygmalion who is praying to Venus for his statue to come to life and (as it indeed did, according to fables of the poets) become flesh and blood."

13. The Ten Thousand Martyrs
64x43 cm
Florence, Uffizi

13

While the *Portrait of Francesco Guardi*, only fifteen or sixteen at the time as he was born to a family in the Santa Croce quarter in 1514, is now in the Getty Museum in Malibu, and absurdly considered by some to be a portrait of Cosimo de' Medici painted around 1537, the "cover," stolen from the Galleria Barberini in Rome during the last war and recovered by Minister Siviero, is now on show at the Uffizi. In the *Pygmalion and Galatea*, a myth drawn from Ovid's *Metamorphoses* and certainly linked in some way to the portrait "in armor" that it covered, Bronzino shows how deep-rooted his ties with Pontormo still were at that time. It was the latter's figures that provided the inspiration for the girl, depicted in a limp pose and with a gloomy expression, and the imploring sculptor, with his eyes staring upward and his hands clasped in prayer. They are reminiscent of similar figures painted by Carrucci around 1518, such as the old woman presented to the Pharaoh in the Borgherini *Joseph in Egypt* in London or the Saint Francis of the *Pucci Altarpiece* in San Michelino Visdomini, in Florence.

This time, however, Agnolo was responsible for the design, as is clear from the rounded forms of the figures rather than the elongation of drapery and members that was typical of Pontormo's work in those years, and from the presence of elements of great originality, such as the sacrificial altar, adorned with figures in high relief and ram's heads, on which burns a docile ox with large dark eyes, and the landscape fading into the darkness of a northern dawn.

14

15. Pygmalion and Galatea
81x64 cm
Florence, Uffizi

In Urbino and during the Reign of Duke Alessandro de' Medici (1530-1536)

"Then with the siege of Florence over, and accord reached, [Bronzino] went, as has been said elsewhere [in the *Life* of Pontormo], to Pesaro, where at the court of Guidobaldo Duke of Urbino he made, in addition to the aforementioned harpsichord case filled with figures, which was a rare thing, a portrait of that lord and of a daughter of Matteo Sofferoni, a painting that was truly beautiful and earned much praise. He also painted some figures in oil on the corbels of a vault in the Imperiale, the duke's villa. And he would have done more if he had not been summoned back to Florence by his master Iacopo Puntormo, to help him finish the hall of Poggio a Caiano." Thus, in a few words in the biography of Bronzino, and at somewhat greater length in the *Life* of Carrucci, Vasari refers to the time the artist

spent in Pesaro in the service of the Della Rovere family. Following the "accord" of August 12, 1530, which sanctioned the city's surrender to the imperial forces, Agnolo left his native city, enticed by the prospect of independent work, as well, it should be added, as by the chance to escape the new outbreak of the plague, brought to Florence by some lansquenets in the imperial army. Among its victims, it was to claim the painter Andrea del Sarto, who died, alone and forsaken, the following September.

Waiting for him in Pesaro was a group of artists from diverse backgrounds, at work since the previous year on the decoration of the eight rooms in the noble apartment of the Villa Imperiale, located two kilometers outside the city walls. They included, in addition to Giro-

16, 17. Portrait of Lady with a Puppy
89x70 cm
Frankfurt, Städelsches Kunstinstitut

with a Puppy in the Städelsches Kunstinstitut in Frankfurt.

The portrait in the German collection, assigned by some experts to Pontormo, is actually one of the finest works of Bronzino's early maturity and stands out for the brilliant and complementary accord between the dark green of the sleeves and the bright red of the dress, recalling the gamut of colors used in the Capponi Chapel or the Pitti *Martyrdom*, and for the sense of Olympian serenity produced by the perfect oval of the subject's luminous face and for the delight in detailed description that is so alien to the style of Pontormo. Perhaps a lady of the Urbino court — to judge by her rich apparel and jewelry — she was not averse to reading, as the two volumes that can be seen behind the lavishly decorated seat indicate.

In the painting in St Petersburg, originally of an irregular shape owing to its use as the lid of a musical instrument, the painter shows, in his depiction of the various episodes in the mythological story, that he has already developed a style of his own, very different from Pontormo's expressionistic distortions. This is also evident in the preparatory drawings for Marsyas playing the flute and King Midas, traced in red pencil on both sides of folio no. 5293 in the Cabinet des Dessins of the Louvre.

The picture in the Galleria Palatina shows us the young hereditary prince (Urbino 1514 - 1574) — the son of Duke Francesco Maria and Duchess Eleonora Gonzaga who just a few years later were portrayed by Titian in the paintings now in the Uffizi — at the age of eighteen, as we are informed by the Latin inscription "ANNUM AGEBAT DECIMUM OCTAVUM" on the table on which his helmet rests. Since Guidobaldo was born on April 2, 1514, it has to be assumed, as Smyth has pointed out, that Bronzino must have begun to paint the portrait on the same date in 1532. This was a particularly important year for the prince, who had been given regency over the duchy while his father was away in Venice.

The young della Rovere is dressed in his new burnished and gilded suit of armor, which Vasari tells us was brought all the way from Lombardy and so desired by the prince that he made the painter wait until it arrived, so that he could be portrayed in this costume of great elegance and refinement. Perhaps a birthday present, it is very different from the rather old-fashioned, "German-style" corselet worn by his father, a celebrated condottiere, in the portrait painted by Vecellio that is now in the Uffizi.

While the expression of the prince, who has an intent gaze and looks as if he were dazzled by the light that makes his face stand out against the background of green cloth, is still reminiscent of Pontormo's portraits, the minute depiction of every detail of the precious cuirass appears to be the work of an already mature artist. Under the breastplate we can glimpse a sleeve of red satin and the hems of an embroidered shirt, while the helmet bears a scroll inscribed with the young man's motto in Greek, indication of an unshakable confidence

lamo Genga, the painter and architect in charge of the undertaking, the brothers Dosso and Battista Dossi, Raffaellino del Colle, Francesco Minzocchi da Forlì, and Camillo Mantovano. Bronzino had to get straight down to work, presumably painting the decorations of the Sala dei Semibusti in partnership with Raffaellino, the other Tuscan, who came originally from Sansepolcro.

However, given the large number of artists involved and the extensive renovations carried out at a later date, it is extremely difficult to establish with sufficient certainty which parts of the murals were actually painted by Bronzino. Nevertheless, paintings in the Sala delle Fatiche d'Ercole and the Main Hall have been attributed to him by Smyth and Marchini. Other records of those lively years in the service of the future Duke of Urbino are the lid of the "harpsichord case," decorated with *The Contest between Apollo and Marsyas* and now in the Hermitage Museum in St Petersburg, the *Portrait of Guidobaldo della Rovere* in the Galleria Palatina in Florence, and, probably, the one of a *Lady*

18, 19. Portrait of Guidobaldo della Rovere
114x86 cm
Florence, Galleria Palatina

19

in his own prowess and determination in matters of arms as well as in the rule of the state: "It will certainly be according to my design."

Leaving the Della Rovere court immediately after the portrait was finished, Bronzino rushed to join Pontormo, who had repeatedly called him to Florence to help him in the task he had been assigned by Ottaviano de' Medici and Duke Alessandro: completing the decoration of the Main Hall of the Medici villa of Poggio a Caiano, left unfinished owing to the death of Franciabigio and Andrea del Sarto.

Notwithstanding the duke's insistence, Pontormo did not get beyond the preparatory drawings and cartoons, which were never put into execution. Work on the now lost decorations of the Medici villa of Careggi, undertaken by Pontormo with the assistance of Bronzino, Jacone, Pierfrancesco di Jacopo Foschi, and other minor collaborators, was also interrupted by the assassination of Alessandro on December 13, 1536.

Between 1532 and 1536 Bronzino also carried out many public and private commissions, painting, among other things, "very fine half-length portraits of Dante, Petrarch, and Boccaccio for Bartolomeo Bettini, to fill some lunettes in one of his bedchambers" (Vasari). It is very likely that one of these figures, now lost and originally accompanied by a *Venus with Cupid* painted by Pontormo to a cartoon by Michelangelo, formed the basis for the *Allegorical Portrait of Dante* in the National Gallery in Washington. One of Bronzino's finest works from the beginning of the 1530s, it is still inexplicably unacknowledged by some critics. The artist, a quite skillful poet in the style of Berni and Petrarch, had in any case long been familiar with the *Divine Comedy*, as indeed were many Florentines of his day. Evidence for this is provided by Varchi's dedication of his translation of the thirteenth book of Ovid's *Metamorphoses*, published in 1539, to Bronzino and Tribolo: "You both delight in and understand poetic things and especially Bronzino who, in addition to his own compositions, has memorized the whole of Dante and a very great deal of Petrarch to a far greater extent than would be believed."

A profound spirituality united with a great moral tension pervades the picture in the American collection. The painter's admiration for the great poet is palpable. He is portrayed with his gaze lifted to the heights of the Kingdom of Heaven and his great book open at the introduction to Canto XXV of the *Paradise*, a sorrowful lament over his exile far from his ungrateful and yet beloved native city, barely visible in the distance on the left.

We also have to concur with Longhi in assigning to Bronzino one of the two versions in Casa Buonarroti of a *Noli me tangere* painted by Pontormo to a cartoon by Michelangelo, in which Buonarroti's design for Christ and Mary Magdalene is clothed in the vivid palette derived from Carrucci and enriched by an ingenious landscape, in which walls and houses climb up a hill, against a night sky rent by a dazzling flicker of light.

During this period Agnolo also did some highly appreciated work as a set designer. In 1533, with the help of Vasari, he painted the "perspective" for a "Comedy of Magicians" performed at the home of Antonio Antinori, and at the same time, according to Vasari, made portraits of many Florentines. One of these, which Vasari erroneously dates to the time of his stay in Urbino, was certainly of a daughter of Matteo Sofferoni. Research carried out by Pilliod has shown her to be the niece of Dianora Sofferoni, the wife of Bronzino's friend the sword-maker Tofano Allori, as well as the mother of his favorite pupil Alessandro. She has been tentatively identified by John Shearman as the subject of the *Portrait of a Woman in a Green Dress* in the Royal Collection at Hampton Court, dating from around 1532.

It was a few years later, probably, that Agnolo painted the *Portrait of a Man with a Lute* in the Uffizi, for which a preparatory study without the musical instrument is known (Chatsworth, Duke of Devonshire Collection, no. 714). This is similar to a study for a *Portrait of a Man* in the Gabinetto Disegni e Stampe of the Uffizi (no. 6698 Florence), wrongly held to be a portrait of Pontormo. The painting in the Uffizi represents a development of the promise shown by the *Portrait of Guidobaldo*, with the use of a similar, intense source of light on the left, that makes the subject's face and hands stand out strongly against the backdrop of a bourgeois interior, the green tablecloth, or the dark garment of rough wool. In an approach to portraiture that was to become typical of Bronzino in the future, the young musician, perhaps a member of Varchi's circle, is depicted as if through a magnifying glass, revealing the tiniest details of his beardless face and strong hands, of the veining of the back of the chair, and of the curious ink pot on the table, in the form of Venus taking a bath, from which projects the tip of a goose quill.

While we do not know the identity of the young man in the Uffizi, we know a great deal about Ugolino Martelli (Florence 1519-1592), portrayed by Bronzino in the picture in the Staatliche Museen in Berlin. This can be dated with certainty to before November 12, 1537, when the young man, a great friend of Varchi's, left Florence for Padua, where he was to stay for five years, keeping the latter company during the exile into which he had been sent because of his republican past.

The slight and sickly adolescent, presumably about seventeen to eighteen years old, is portrayed during a pause in his reading of the Greek text of the ninth book of the *Iliad*, with the book open on the table and his finger marking the point where he had broken off. He is holding a text by Bembo against his left thigh, in an affected pose, while a volume of Virgil can be glimpsed on his left. Both are recognizable by the Latin writing on the spine and pages and are intended to underline the refined culture and humanistic erudition of the young prodigy, who was praised on several occasions by Varchi, Aretino, and Bembo.

In the background, at the end of a row of windows seen in perspective that evokes the courtyard of his ancestral palace, the *Martelli David* stands on a plinth.

The pride of the family collections, it was formerly attributed to Donatello and is now thought to be the work of one of the Rossellino brothers (Washington, National Gallery).

It is likely that the last of the three portraits of young men was the *Portrait of a Youth with a Book* in the Metropolitan Museum in New York, painted between 1537 and 1539. Radiographic examination of the work, described by Cox Rearick in 1982, reveals that both the background and the figure underwent significant revisions during the execution.

A new maturity of expression and technique emerges

20. Allegorical Portrait of Dante
127x120 cm
Washington, National Gallery of Art

from the depiction of the smooth skin, as white as ivory, and of the costly black fabric of his fashionable clothing, offering a foretaste of the typical icy refinements of the portraits that Bronzino was to paint in the fifth decade of the sixteenth century.

21, 22. Noli me tangere
172x134 cm
Florence, Casa Buonarroti

23

23. Portrait of Young Man with a Lute
98x82.5 cm
Florence, Uffizi

24. Portrait of Ugolino Martelli
102x85 cm
Berlin, Staatliche Museen

In these same years, marked by the killing of Duke Alessandro by his cousin Lorenzino and the coming to power of the young Cosimo, the son of Giovanni dalle Bande Nere and Maria Salviati, Bronzino painted the precious *Adoration of the Shepherds* in the Szép-müvészeti Múzeum in Budapest for Filippo di Averardo Salviati. Engraved by Giorgio Ghisi in 1554, it draws on an eclectic range of sources: elements still in the style of Pontormo, such as the long-limbed Madonna at the center of the composition, are combined with the well-turned bodies of the shepherds, derived from studies of the ancients, depicted in the palette of bright and glowing colors that he was to use for the panels and frescoes of Eleonora of Toledo's Chapel in the Palazzo Vecchio.

25. Portrait of Young Man with a Lute, detail, ink pot in the form of Venus taking a bath Florence, Uffizi

26. Portrait of Ugolino Martelli, detail, the Martelli David Berlin, Staatliche Museen

Official Painter and Portraitist of the Medici Court (1537-1555)

As was the custom, the wedding of Cosimo I de' Medici (Florence 1519-1574) and the Spaniard Eleonora of Toledo (Naples 1522-Pisa 1562), daughter of the Viceroy of Naples, was accompanied by a sumptuous display to celebrate the bride's entry into the city, on June 29, 1539, with works of mock architecture set up at particular points of the city. For this auspicious event, held in the great court of Palazzo Medici on Via Larga, Aristotile da Sangallo prepared a hall to be used for the banquet and a stage for the performance of Antonio Landi's play *Il Commodo*. The walls of the room were decorated with twelve scenes, six of them devoted to the Medici of the fifteenth and sixteenth century and the rest to celebration of the new duke. They were painted by the greatest artists of the day, with the exception of Pontormo, at that time engaged with Bronzino on the decoration of a loggia in the Medici villa of Castello (1537-1543). Along with Bachiacca, Foschi, Domenico Conti, Antonio di Donnino, Battista Franco, and Salviati, who was assisted by Portelli, Bronzino could not fail to make a contribution. Indeed, he took the lead, depicting the "dispute that took place between Duke Alessandro and the Florentine exiles before the emperor in Naples [in 1536], with the Sebeto river and many figures." According to Vasari, this was a "beautiful picture, and better than all the others [...]" and was accompanied by "the wedding of Duke Cosimo himself held in Naples [on March 29, 1539]...," a work "done with such grace that it surpasses, like the first, all the other scenes" (Vasari). These temporary and unfortunately long vanished paintings aroused great admiration, as did the two scenes in mock bronze on the plinth of Tribolo's equestrian statue of Giovanni dalle Bande Nere set up in Piazza San Marco. With them, the painter had quite unwittingly made his fortune, "and the duke, realizing the quality of this man, set him to work in his ducal palace on a not very large chapel for the said lady duchess, who was truly one of the most outstanding women there has ever been, and worthy of eternal praise for her infinite merits" (Vasari).

Unlike his predecessors, Cosimo had in fact chosen to move out of the family palace and into the Palazzo della Signoria, the illustrious seat of the Priors and the republican magistrates since the end of the thirteenth century, in order to "show that he was absolute prince, and arbiter of the Government, and dishearten those who presumed, as had happened other times, that the rule of the city be separated from that of the Medici family" (Adriani).

On May 15, 1540, while work was still proceeding on the adaptation of the medieval building with its tower, under the supervision of the engraver and court architect Battista del Tasso, the duke moved in, together with his consort, their firstborn daughter Maria, and the court. Although they did not take up permanent residence until 1542, he took steps right from the start to make the palace comfortable for his beloved Eleonora, to whom he may have given, as Simon supposes, his own *Portrait as Orpheus*, painted by Bronzino and now in the Philadelphia Museum of Art, as a token of his love.

The duchess was assigned the most private rooms on the second floor, previously occupied by the Priors and the Gonfalonier of Justice, while the duke took those on the *piano nobile*, on the same level as the Salone dei Cinquecento, formerly used by Gonfalonier Soderini.

After Tasso had constructed the small space of the chapel and the so-called "Camera Verde", which by 1542 had been decorated with grotesques by Ridolfo del Ghirlandaio, Bronzino must have commenced work. It is likely that he prepared the designs and cartoons in 1540 and started to fresco the vault at the beginning of the following year, as was the customary practice.

The ceiling was illusionistically divided by four festoons supported by putti against the background of a clear and bright sky. On fleecy clouds, he set *Saint Michael the Archangel defeating the Demon*, *Saint Francis receiving the Stigmata*, *Saint Jerome in Penitence*, and *Saint John the Evangelist on Patmos*, painted in a symphony of lapis-lazuli blues, vivid and brilliant reds, and intense yellows, laid on with such great care that he made the rapid technique of the fresco resemble the refined painting on board typical of his work in those years, characterized by the use of glowing colors. The painting had been preceded by a phase of careful preparation, from which, along with the many drawings that were certainly made and a nude study for the figure of *Saint Michael* (Paris, Louvre, Cabinet des Dessins no. 6356), the precious small-scale design for the ceiling survives. In pen and ink on light-blue paper with highlights in white lead and now in the Städelsches Kunstinstitut in Frankfurt (no. 4344), it was undoubtedly made for presentation to the duke and duchess in order to obtain their indispensable approval.

Having finished the ceiling, adorned at the center with a Medici-Toledo coat of arms, now barely visible under the later Trinitarian symbol of the "Vultus trifrons" in a garland of flowers, added by Bronzino himself in 1565, the artist moved onto the decoration of the walls, for which records exist of payments made between 1542 and 1544, though these make no reference to the actual works involved. He started work on the *Crossing of the Red Sea* on the wall opposite the window, which took the unusually long time of seven months to be completed, from September 6, 1541, to March 30, 1542. This information is supplied by some sixteenth-century inscriptions in an anonymous hand on the inner frame of the chapel's marble door, which was probably carved to a design by Tasso.

This fresco reveals the vast range of Agnolo's figurative culture, which allowed him to combine borrowings from Michelangelo with citations from the classical repertoire. An example of the latter is the pose of the

*27. Design for the ceiling of the Chapel
of Eleonora
343x262 mm
Frankfurt, Städelsches Kunstinstitut, no. 4344*

*28. Chapel of Eleonora, ceiling
490x385 cm
Florence, Palazzo Vecchio*

29. *View of the Chapel of Eleonora*
Florence, Palazzo Vecchio

30, 31. *The Crossing of the Red Sea*
320x490 cm
Florence, Palazzo Vecchio

32. *The Crossing of the Red Sea, detail*
Florence, Palazzo Vecchio

33. *Study of nude for the Crossing of*
the Red Sea
420x155 mm
Florence, Uffizi, Gabinetto Disegni e Stampe,
no. 6704 F

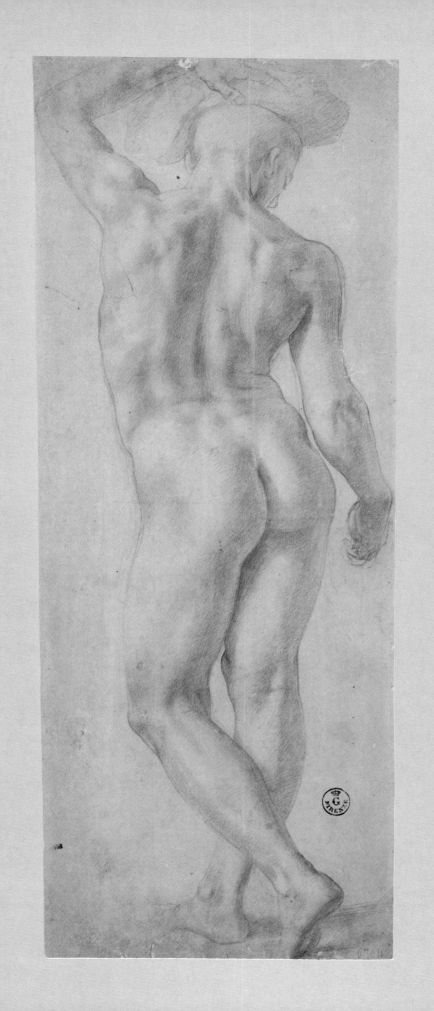

figure of a youth with a bundle of clothes on his head, represented from behind on the left and derived, as Smyth has pointed out, from the bronze statue known as the *Idolino* (Florence, Museo Archeologico) that had been found at the Imperial Villa in Pesaro in 1530. The splendid nude drawing in the Uffizi (no. 6704 Florence), traced in black pencil on paper primed with yellow, is a study of this statuette. Among the many figures that throng the crowded Biblical scene, Bronzino chose to portray, in an act of homage and set almost in the middle of the composition, the duke's all-powerful major-domo and secretary Pierfrancesco Riccio (Prato 1499 - Florence 1564). Riccio served as the intermediary between Cosimo de' Medici and the artists, who owed everything to his favor, as Francesco Salviati was to learn to his cost several years later, falling into disfavor at the court precisely because he had made an enemy of him by his "choleric and mordant nature" (Vasari).

The next part of the chapel to be frescoed was the entrance wall, with the *Worship of the Brazen Serpent*. This was begun, according to the aforementioned inscriptions, on June 5, 1542, and probably finished within the year. Such a highly dramatic subject provided

34, 35. The Worship of the Brazen Serpent
320x385 cm
Florence, Palazzo Vecchio

the artist with the opportunity for an exciting composition along the lines of Michelangelo's *terribilità* in the *Last Judgment*, with virtuoso foreshortenings of naked bodies struggling with snakes, inspired by classical statuary, in a gamut of colors as dazzling as the light that shines on them from the cross with a serpent wrapped round it, placed at the center of the composition.

Immediately afterward, presumably between the end of 1542 and the beginning of 1543, the artist moved on to the wall with the window, which is flanked by two more episodes from the cycle representing the life of the great lawgiver and liberator of the people of Israel: on the left he painted *Moses striking Water from the Rock* and, on the right, *The Collection of Manna*. They are separated by two *Small Angels with a Chalice and a Globe*, a later intervention by Alessandro Allori, dating from the years 1581-2 when the window was trans-

formed into a door providing access to the terrace and to the workroom above the Dogana, adorned with grotesques by Tommaso di Battista del Verrocchio.

In the first fresco, beneath the figure of Moses working the miracle, the thirsty Jews scramble over each other to get to the flowing water, with elements of great realism such as the desperate crying of the little boy clinging to the neck of his mother while she draws water from the spring, behind naked youths stretching over the pool of water. In the second, on the other hand, the other figures are dominated by a young man on the left, bent beneath the weight of a large pot filled with manna, while men and women behind him gather up the fruit of the prodigious and unseasonable snowfall by any means available. Connected with these frescoes, there is a study for the head of the woman on the far left, in the Louvre (no. 17), a drawing of the next two male figures, in the Uffizi (no. 10320 F recto), and a study for the young man in the *Collection of the Manna* at the Pinacoteca Ambrosiana in Milan (Resta Codex no. 48).

Finally the painter turned his attention to the decoration of the altar wall, frescoing the *Prophet David* and the *Erythraean Sibyl* in segments at the top. They were probably painted, according to Cox-Rearick, at the beginning of 1543, as was the fresco of the *Justice* in the pendentive of the vault. The other pendentives, with the Virtues of *Prudence*, *Temperance*, and *Fortitude*, were

36. Moses striking Water from the Rock and the Collection of Manna
320x150 cm (left panel); 320x160 cm (right panel)
Florence, Palazzo Vecchio

37. The Collection of Manna, detail
Florence, Palazzo Vecchio

not executed until 1565, and were painted *a secco*.

However Agnolo put his greatest effort into the altarpiece with the *Deposition*. In 1542 Baccio Bandinelli had unfairly sought to obtain the commission for this work for himself, by presenting the duke and duchess with an overall design which so pleased Eleonora that it was decided to have Bronzino turn it into a painting. Contrary to the view of Cox-Rearick, who sees unlikely affinities between Bronzino's and Bandinelli's figures, Agnolo was obliged, against his will, to adopt his rival's idea, but limited himself to making use of its composition and not the details.

The result of Bronzino's work was so magnificent, as is apparent when one sees the panel, now in the Musée des Beaux-Arts in Besançon, that Nicolas Perrenot de Granvelle, the influential private secretary to Emperor Charles V with whom Cosimo was negotiating for the return of the fortresses of Pisa and Livorno, occupied by Spanish garrisons, desired to obtain it for himself.

So it was that the altarpiece, which must have been finished by July 15, 1545, the date when the gilder of the frame was paid, only spent two months on the chapel's altar before being sent, the following September, to Besançon, the imperial dignitary's native city, to be set up in his chapel in the Carmelite church.

The *Deposition*, which was not replaced on the altar of the chapel until 1553 and then only by a replica of lesser quality by the same artist, is such as to make one truly regret Cosimo's forced decision to relinquish it "for reasons of state," so perfect is the drawing of Christ's ivory-white body and so precious the details and the richness of the glowing colors, laid over a priming as smooth as marble and in a palette that tends to favor bluish tones, as in the sky surrounded by clouds in which five chubby little angels hover with the instruments of the Passion. The only record, in our current state of knowledge, of the customary, careful phase of preparation for the picture, is provided by the study for the face of the devout woman behind the Virgin, conserved in the Uffizi (no. 10894 F). An unhappy fate also befell the two side panels that went with it, depicting *Saint John the Baptist* (Malibu, Getty Museum) and *Saint Cosmas*, now lost, which were replaced in 1564 by the *Announcing Angel* and *Our Lady of the Annunciation* that are still in place, after being removed from the chapel at the duchess's behest and put away in the ducal wardrobe, where their presence was recorded as early as 1553.

Perhaps for Eleonora of Toledo and probably during the final stage of the work on the chapel or shortly before it, the artist also painted a small *Annunciation*. An engraving of this was made by Hieronimus Cock in the middle of the sixteenth century and is now on show in the Tribuna of the Uffizi. Although it is in need of a light cleaning, the panel displays the preciosity of Bronzino's best work and a light and luminous range of colors like that of the frescoes in Palazzo Vecchio.

The unusual length of time required for the decoration of the chapel, a total of five years, should be ascribed not only to the perfectionism and meticulousness typical of Bronzino, which required him to work at an extremely slow pace, but also to a series of interruptions due to the numerous commissions he received in the capacity that was to earn him real fame, that of official portrait painter of the Medici and of members of other noble families with ties to their court.

In the forties and fifties of the sixteenth century, Bronzino was in fact called on to portray, on several occasions, not just the duke and duchess but also the eight children born from their fertile union, starting in 1540, the year of birth of their eldest daughter Maria, and lasting up until 1554, that of their youngest son Piero. However the first portrait he painted was of an illegitimate daughter of Cosimo's, the little Bia who died while still a child in February 1542. She is portrayed with a tiny medal round her neck bearing the effigy of her still youthful father, in the small panel hanging in the Tribuna of the Uffizi. It was followed by two portraits, again in the Uffizi, of Giovanni de' Medici (Florence 1543-

37

38. *Moses striking Water from the Rock, detail*
Florence, Palazzo Vecchio

39. *The Collection of Manna, detail*
Florence, Palazzo Vecchio

Livorno 1562), in one of which he appears by himself before the end of 1544, to judge by the presumable age of the child, who is laughing and showing two milk teeth — which were emerging in the summer of that year — and clutching a goldfinch in his chubby little hand, against his rich red garment, and in the other with his mother Eleonora, at the age of two, and therefore painted by the summer of 1545. At that time Bronzino was staying at the Medici villa of Poggio a Caiano to paint the pictures of "our Angels," as he called them in a letter to Riccio dated August 9, 1545, the little princesses and princes Maria (Florence 1540-57), Francesco (Florence 1541-87), Isabella (Florence 1542-Cerreto Guidi 1576), Lucrezia (Florence 1545-Ferrara 1561) and Giovanni. The latter was the second-born son, always cheerful, and, in all likelihood, his mother's favorite. In the letter, the painter seems to be referring to the double portrait in the Uffizi when he asks for more ultramarine paint made from lapis lazuli, adding "[...] for I think I cannot do with less, since the ground is large and has to be dark," just as the background of sky above the landscape that fades into the distance behind Eleonora and her little son is large and dark. Cosimo's wife, her beautiful oval face lit up against the stormy sky, had herself portrayed in her finest dress, made of white damask cloth and adorned with pearls and gold trimmings, and in her richest jewelry, includ-

40. Annunciation, Deposition of Christ, the Prophet David and the Erythraean Sibyl (Chapel of Eleonora, end wall)
Florence, Palazzo Vecchio

41. Deposition of Christ
268x173 cm
Besançon, Musée des Beaux-Arts

42, 43. Deposition of Christ, details
Besançon, Musée des Beaux-Arts

44. Study for the face of the devout woman
in the Deposition of Christ
156x164 mm
Florence, Uffizi, Gabinetto Disegni e Stampe,
no. 10894 F

45. Deposition of Christ, detail, the devout woman
behind the Virgin
Besançon, Musée des Beaux-Arts

ing a belt studded with precious stones. Her mother-in-law, Maria Salviati (Florence 1499-1543), the widow of Giovanni dalle Bande Nere to whom the little children were often entrusted, had also been portrayed by Bronzino shortly before her death, which took place on December 20, 1543. The picture, currently in the De Young Memorial Museum in San Francisco, was later used for her funeral.

The other portraits of the Medici children that have come down to us date from a later period, the years 1550-1, when Bronzino went to Pisa to paint the pictures of Maria, the eldest, at the age of around eleven, and Francesco, ten years old, both now in the Uffizi, along with a lost portrait of Giovanni, aged seven and already destined for the cardinalate, which was donated to Pope Julius III, a portrait of Garzia (Florence 1547-Pisa 1562) at the age of three, perhaps to be identified with a painting in the Prado, and many other replicas, mentioned in the correspondence with Riccio.

While we also have a portrait of the duchess just after she was married, now in the National Gallery of Prague, and several others, at an advanced age and worn-out by sickness, the most popular picture of the duke was a portrait "in armor" that was endlessly reproduced by the workshop. Only two completely autograph versions of it are known, the half-length one in the Uffizi and a second, three-quarter-length one, in a British private collection and in any case painted prior to August 11, 1545, owing to the absence of the Order of the Golden Fleece, which the emperor bestowed on the duke on that date.

With the establishment of the Medici tapestry factory in 1543, at the behest of Cosimo, Bronzino was given almost total responsibility, between 1545 and 1553, for the factory's major undertaking, designing sixteen of the twenty tapestries in the series of *Scenes from the Life of Joseph the Patriarch* (Depositories of the Florentine Galleries, currently undergoing restoration) that were woven by the Flemings Jan Rost and Nicolas Karcher to decorate the Salone de' Dugento in Palazzo Vecchio. He was given the job after the unsuccessful attempt by Pontormo, who should be considered responsible for the design of the three tapestries now in the Quirinal, and the limited contribution made by Francesco Salviati, in Florence from 1543 to 1548, who produced the cartoon for only one tapestry, representing *Joseph explaining the Dream of the Fat Kine and the Lean Kine to the Pharaoh*.

Although the latter was a brilliant and revolutionary artist, as the frescoes in the Audience Chamber and in Eleonora's Study in the Palazzo Vecchio testify, he was often passed over for Bronzino. An example of this is the tapestry portiere depicting *Justice liberating Innocence* (Depositories of the Florentine Galleries), for which we have a design by Salviati, in the Uffizi and the cartoon by Bronzino (Milan, Biblioteca Ambrosiana, Resta Codex) that was actually used by Rost to weave the tapestry by the spring of 1546, along with the other portiere, again to Bronzino's design, with *Flora* or the *Spring* (Depositories of the Florentine Galleries).

From the forties onward, however busy with the duke's commissions, the artist managed to combine them with an intense activity as a portrait painter for families of the nobility and upper middle class, from both Florence and elsewhere. Surviving examples of these are the *Portrait of a Young Lady with her Child* in the National Gallery in Washington, perhaps a princess from the House of Este or of Gonzaga to judge by the peculiar style of the precious headgear she is wearing, and the *Portrait of a Young Girl with a Prayer Book* in the Uffizi, painted between 1541 and 1545.

Bronzino also worked for noblemen and cultured gentlemen drawn to the Medici court, such as the rich merchant of Pistoian origin, Bartolomeo Panciatichi (Lyons? 1507-Pistoia 1582), whose appearance was captured forever in the picture in the Uffizi. This shows him at the age of about thirty-six to thirty-seven, in an elegant black garment depicted by the painter with infinite "pains," down to the smallest details of the "cut" sleeves, against a backdrop of quite distinct buildings, from which the family coat of arms stands out. This can also be seen on the red standard that flies from the tower of an unknown city set in the background of the *Holy Family* in the Uffizi, one of two pictures of this subject which the artist painted for Panciatichi according to Vasari and imbued with an affectionate air by the touching image of the kiss that the young St John is giving to the Christ Child, asleep on a precious blue cushion.

As a companion piece to the portrait of Bartolomeo, Agnolo painted one of his wife Lucrezia di Gismondo Pucci (Florence ?-1572), whom he married in 1534. Apparently much younger than her husband, she is swathed in a rich dress of rustling satin and brilliantly illuminated against the dark ground of the architecture. She is holding open a "Breviary of the Virgin" with her left hand and displaying her rich jewelry, including a long gold chain with enameled segments making up the French motto "Amour dure sans fin," an allusion to the fidelity and affection of her husband.

The use of the French language is explained by the fact that Panciatichi had spent the whole of his youth in Lyons, where the family, like many other Florentines, had a house and a warehouse that they used for trading, and had served as a page to Francis I. It was probably he and not Duke Cosimo, as has wrongly been thought, who commissioned from Bronzino the painting "of singular beauty, that was sent to King Francis in France; in which there was a naked Venus with Cupid kissing her, and Pleasure on one side and Play with other Loves, and on the other Deceit, Jealousy, and other amorous passions" (Vasari). To Vasari's description, fairly vague perhaps because it was based on memory, should be added the figure of Time as Saturn, the father of all vice, set at the top right, with the attributes of an hourglass and wings, looking at Deceit, on the other side, who is helping him to hold up the large blue drape. Behind Cupid, who is kissing his mother Venus, are set, from left to right, Jealousy screaming with her hands in her hair, Play scattering rose petals and wearing bells around her left ankle but, at the same time, with her right foot pierced by sharp thorns, and Pleasure, symbolized by a

46. Annunciation
57x43.5 cm
Florence, Uffizi

young girl with the body of a serpent and the feet of a lion, who is offering a honeycomb with one hand and concealing a scorpion's sting in the other. The result is a refined allegory of Profane Love, of its skirmishes and deceptions. This was a theme well suited to the august recipient and in tune with the chill sensuality of the naked ladies in the pictures of the School of Fontainebleau.

The picture, now in the National Gallery in London, must have been painted by Bronzino before 1545, the year of the French king's death, and may have been based on an erudite idea from Panciatichi himself, a well-versed man of letters and since 1541 a member of the recently established Accademia Fiorentina, or from Luigi Alamanni, at the French court at that time and certainly in contact with cultural circles in Florence.

Bronzino himself, moreover, was quite capable of interpreting such cultivated ideas, thanks to a culture that was not common among the artists of his day. Evidence for this comes not only from his lofty sonnets in the

mold of Petrarch, but also from licentious poetic compositions in the style of Berni, such as the *Capitolo del Pennello*, published in 1538 and full of mischievous allusions of an erotic and homosexual character.

Joining the Accademia degli Umidi, later the Accademia Fiorentina, in 1541, along with Tribolo, he remained a member for six years until his expulsion following its reform, in 1547, attending the lectures, chiefly on the works of Dante and Petrarch, the glories of Florence, and associating with the finest minds of his time. Among them were his friend Varchi, who had returned from exile in 1543, the young Ugolino Martelli, and many other scholars, including Gelli and Giambullari, whom he portrayed in 1550 among the bystanders in the *Descent of Christ into Limbo* in Santa Croce.

On November 19, 1542, the Roman condottiere Stefano Colonna (Rome c. 1490-Pisa 1548), whom Cosimo I had made Lieutenant-General of the ducal army, was also admitted to the Accademia, along with

47. *Portrait of Bia de' Medici*
63x48 cm
Florence, Uffizi

48. *Portrait of Maria de' Medici as a Girl*
52.5x38 cm
Florence, Uffizi

49. *Portrait of Francesco de' Medici as a Child*
58.5x41.5 cm
Florence, Uffizi

50. *Portrait of Giovanni de' Medici as a Child*
58x45.6 cm
Florence, Uffizi

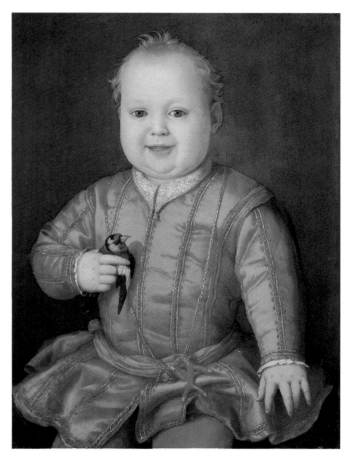

51. Portrait of Eleonora of Toledo with her Son Giovanni
115x96 cm
Florence, Uffizi

52. *Portrait of Cosimo I
in Armor
71x57 cm
Florence, Uffizi*

his son Francesco. In 1546 Bronzino painted a proud and martial picture of him, encased in his black armor chased with gold and decorated with the family coat of arms. While this portrait, now in the Galleria Nazionale d'Arte Antica in Rome, is lively and realistic in its approach, the *Portrait of Andrea Doria as Neptune* (Milano, Brera) is allegorical in its conception and idealizing in its intent. The picture of Doria (Oneglia 1466-Genoa 1560) took its inspiration from a monument by Bandinelli and was painted for the Museum of Paolo Giovio in Como, presumably between 1546 and 1548.

This was probably also the period in which the artist painted the *Holy Family with Saint Anne and the Young Saint John* in the Kunsthistorisches Museum in Vienna, of which a later copy, executed mainly by his studio, is now in the Louvre. The person who commissioned the picture, groundlessly claimed by some to have been the physicist Francesco da Montevarchi, will only be known if the owner of the towered villa in the background, located outside the walls, can be identified.

When, along with other artists, he was asked by Varchi in 1547 which of the two Arts, Painting and Sculpture, was the greatest, Bronzino replied with a letter that was never finished. After much learned argumentation, the letter did not reach a conclusion, although it is easy to presume that it would have been in favor of Painting.

Between April 8, 1548, the date on which the contract for the altarpiece depicting the *Resurrection* for the Guadagni Chapel in the church of Santissima Annunziata was drawn up, and the 27th of the same month, the artist went to Rome for unknown reasons. He borrowed twenty scudi from Duke Cosimo for the purpose, paying them back later, at his own request, a little at a time.

However he did not cease to carry out his much-ap-

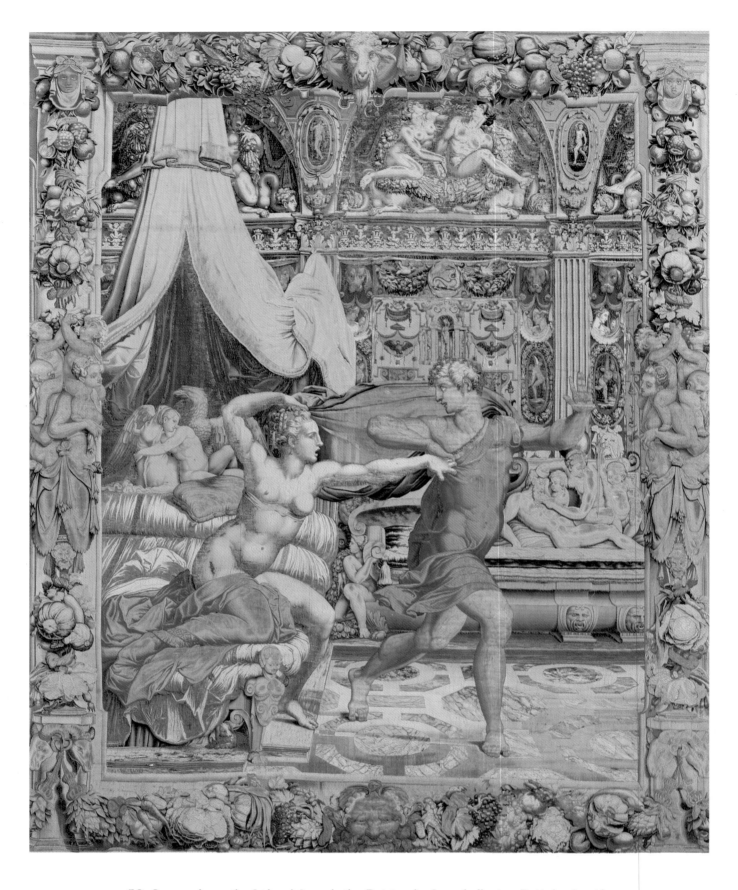

53. Scenes from the Life of Joseph the Patriarch: Joseph fleeing Potiphar's wife
570x457 cm
Florence, Palazzo Vecchio

54. Joseph allowing Himself to be Recognized by his Brothers
556x450 cm
Florence, Palazzo Vecchio

55. Justice liberating Innocence
242x172 cm
Depositories of the Florentine Galleries

preciated activity as a portrait painter, as is attested by such works from the end of the fifth decade as the *Portrait of a Gentleman* in the National Gallery in Ottawa, whose slight resemblance to Cosimo de' Medici does not seem sufficient to justify its being considered a portrait of the duke, as some have done in the past, or the *Portrait of a Gentlewoman* in the Galleria Sabauda in Turin. The latter has often been claimed to be a picture of Eleonora of Toledo, on the basis of a similarity of measurements, but in all probability is a portrait of a wealthy lady of the Florentine aristocracy in her opulent silk clothes, painted, along with the striped fabric in the background, with "a clarity of 'values' worthy of a Dutch painter of the following century" (Longhi).

The portrait of the seventeen-year-old Ludovico Capponi (Florence 1534 - 1614) in the Frick Collection in New York, accustomed to love affairs in spite of his tender age, as is suggested by the miniature cameo portrait concealed in his right hand, and dressed in black-and-white clothes that allude to the colors of his family's coat of arms, set against a large piece of cloth in a bright shade of green, should be dated to around 1551.

A mannered affectation very different from the perfection of the *Allegory* in London is displayed by the

56. Portrait of Young Girl with a Prayer Book
58x46.5 cm
Florence, Uffizi

57. Portrait of Bartolomeo Panciatichi
104x84 cm
Florence, Uffizi

58. Portrait of Lucrezia Panciatichi
102x85 cm
Florence, Uffizi

panel depicting *Venus, Cupid, and Jealousy* in the Szépmüvészeti Múzeum in Budapest, signed but executed largely by the workshop, in which the best parts are the grotesque masks and the partly withered flowers, and by the one with *Venus, Cupid, and a Satyr* (Rome, Galleria Colonna), painted for Alamanno Salviati, both of them dating from 1550-5.

The altarpieces on a religious theme that he painted in these years are also unnecessarily complicated and intricate compositions. They include the Guadagni *Resurrection* in the church of the Nunziata, which had a very long period of gestation, from 1548 to 1552, and the *Descent of Christ into Limbo*, executed by 1552 for the Zanchini altar in Santa Croce and made interesting only by the presence of many portraits of Florentine artists, men of letters, and citizens. Among them, Vasari lists Pontormo, Bachiacca, Gelli, Giovambattista Doni's wife Costanza da Sommaia, and Cammilla Tebaldi del Corno. Even paintings of a small size like the *Saint John the Baptist* in the Galleria Borghese in Rome, with its forced and affected treatment of the limbs, and the *Madonna and Child with the Young Saint John and the Lamb* (Portland Art Museum) confirm that the artist's vein of creativity had partially run dry. Now conditioned by his admiration for Buonarroti, his work was increasingly distant from the balance and harmony he had achieved at the peak of his career, in the fifteen forties.

58

61, 62. Allegory of Venus and Cupid
146x116 cm
London, National Gallery

63. *Portrait of Andrea Doria as Neptune*
115x53 cm
Milan, Pinacoteca di Brera

64. *Portrait of Stefano Colonna*
125x95 cm
Rome, Galleria Nazionale di Arte Antica

65. *Portrait of a Gentlewoman*
109x85 cm
Turin, Galleria Sabauda

66. *Portrait of Ludovico Capponi*
116.5x86 cm
New York, Frick Collection

The Late Works (1556-1572)

Although the recipient of the duke's beneficence in 1551 and regularly inscribed in the roll of those paid a salary by his court in 1553, Bronzino lost the role of chief court painter that he had had for the last fifteen years on the arrival of Vasari, who in 1555 was given the job of decorating the state apartments and the Salone dei Cinquecento in Palazzo Vecchio. While the artist from Arezzo was on his way to becoming the arbiter of the artistic scene in Florence and the recipient of the main ducal commissions, Agnolo painted the canvas that depicts the *Dwarf Morgante* on both sides (Florence, Depositories of the Florentine Galleries, currently under restoration) and concluded his collaboration with the Medici tapestry factory with the cartoons for four more tapestries depicting scenes from Ovid's *Metamorphoses* (1555-8), of which the *Contest between Apollo and Marsyas* survives in the Galleria Nazionale of Parma. For Cosimo de' Medici he also painted the

Portrait of Piero the Gouty (London, National Gallery) and, with considerable help from the workshop, twenty-five *Small Portraits of the Medici* on tin (Florence, Galleria degli Uffizi), which in 1568 the duke guarded jealously, along with other miniature portraits, antique medals, small bronzes, and jewelry, in the Scrittoio di Calliope located in the Quartiere degli Elementi of the Palazzo Vecchio.

On the other hand Bronzino did not have the makings either of the "painter of history" or of the flattering and obsequious artist that Vasari was, two requisites that were well suited to the duke's new needs. Having recently triumphed over Siena and now the ruler of a strong and well-organized state, he wanted to legitimize his authority as the illustrious descendant of the Medici of the fifteenth and early sixteenth century, "those earthly gods of the Medici House" who were later to be celebrated by Vasari and his collaborators in the rooms

67, 68. Allegory of Happiness
40x30 cm
Florence, Uffizi

of the Quartiere di Leone X (Palazzo Vecchio).

Cosimo certainly did not forget his faithful servant Agnolo, but continued to give him commissions in the city and the state, such as the completion of the frescoes in the chancel of San Lorenzo, left unfinished in 1557 on the death of Pontormo, whose natural heir he in any case was. Other commissions included the *Nativity* for the church of Santo Stefano dei Cavalieri in Pisa (dated 1564) and the large altarpiece representing the *Pietà* (Florence, Galleria dell'Accademia) painted for the Monastery of the Observant Franciscans in Cosmopoli (now Portoferraio). Like the *Announcing Angel* and *Our Lady of the Annunciation* for Eleonora of Toledo's chapel in Palazzo Vecchio, this was completed by 1565 and followed, a few years later, by the fresco of the *Martyrdom of Saint Lawrence* in the left-hand aisle of the church of San Lorenzo, patronized by the Medici.

On the occasion of the stately marriage between Prince Francesco de' Medici and Joan of Austria in 1565, the artist, now aged sixty-two, was entrusted with the three canvases of the arch erected on the front of Palazzo Ricasoli at the Ponte alla Carraia, dedicated to Hymen. Two studies for these have come down to us, one depicting the *Allegory of Marriage with Apollo and the Muses* (Paris, Musée du Louvre, no. 953) and another the *Virtues of Love driving out the Vices* (Oxford, Christ Church, no. 1340).

It was a precise intention to build up a collection, on the other hand, that lay behind the painting on copper representing the *Allegory of Happiness*, in the Uffizi. It was commissioned from Bronzino in 1564 by the prince regent, Francesco de' Medici, along with the *Forge of Vulcan* by Vasari (Florence, Uffizi) and other small paintings ordered from various artists, including members of the youngest generation, in a sort of "dress

71. Saint Andrew
159.5x89.5 cm
Rome, Accademia di San Luca

72. Saint Bartholomew
155x93 cm
Rome, Accademia di San Luca

rehearsal" for the decoration of the "Studiolo" in the Palazzo Vecchio.

Bronzino had by now been living for a long time, presumably ever since the forties, with his mother Felice and niece Diamante at the home of the Allori family on Corso degli Adimari (now Via dei Calzaiuoli), close to the Cathedral. Cristofano, the head of the household and a very close friend of Bronzino's, was often so ill that he was unable to maintain his family and Agnolo had always helped him out with money. On his death, in 1541, the artist took his place, looking after the widow, Dianora Sofferoni, and the children Alessandra, Lorenzo, Bastiano, and Alessandro.

Bronzino, who lived in the cramped quarters of a room only three braccia long (about one meter seventy-five centimeters), as he tells us in the burlesque poem entitled "I Romori," devoted to his friend Luca Martini and written during a brief indisposition from which they both suffered during the summer of an unspecified year, had to cope with the difficulties of living with a large number of people, in a densely populated city. He was tormented by the noises and smells that rose from the leather and hosiery workshops in the street nearby, as well as by the continuous ringing of the bells that in those days used to mark every hour and event of the day ("Capitolo contro le campane," written at the Villa of Poggio a Caiano in August 1545 with a dedication to Martini).

For this reason the artist, a poet for his own pleasure and that of his friends, was forced to write his verses at night, when he was finally at peace and free from the demands of painting, as he notes in the burlesque poem "Delle scuse": "Everything is fine, I admit: but if I stay up / much of the night and sleep little, / and only choose that time for my rhymes, / what should I do? Then I build, and shape / castles in the air, and grow bored with idleness, [...]."

In the years from 1555 to 1560 the painter had five of his *Capitoli*, or burlesque poems, printed, including the two dedicated to his friend Luca Martini and one to Benedetto Varchi (1555), the fourteen *Saltarelli* in defense of Annibal Caro against Ludovico Castelvetro (1558-9), and four sonnets that were published together with verses by the poetess Laura Battiferri (1560).

Of the latter, to whom he had addressed some of his sonnets, Agnolo painted one of his most penetrating portraits. Now in the Loeser Collection in Palazzo Vecchio, it was celebrated by Anton Francesco Grazzini, called Il Lasca, in verses full of praise and admiration for both the subject and the skill of the artist.

This cultured gentlewoman (Urbino 1523-Florence 1589), who had married the sculptor and architect Bartolomeo Ammannati on April 17, 1550, and had an intellectual stature that was far from common among the women of her time, was preserved for posterity with an expression rapt in meditation on a book of the lyric poems of Petrarch, which she is holding open with her long, slender hands at sonnets LXIV, "Se voi poteste per turbati segni," and CCXL, "I'ho pregato Amor, ne'l riprego," certainly her favorites and well known to the painter, who accurately transcribed them in his fine and clear handwriting.

The elongated limbs and the use of Pontormo's late manner seem to indicate that the portrait was painted around 1557-8, at the time when Bronzino was commissioned to complete the frescoes in San Lorenzo. The ones that he finished were the *Flood*, the *Resurrection of the Dead*, and a *Martyrdom of St Lawrence* (Vasari), conforming, as far as we can tell from surviving drawings like the study for the *Blessing of Noah's Seed* (London, British Museum, no. 1794.4.6.36), to the style of his beloved master. Bronzino still saw him regularly, often inviting him to dinner, usually on a Sunday, as Pontormo recorded in the diary that he kept during the last years of his life (1554-6).

It is to this period or shortly afterward that the *Portrait of a Young Man with a Plumed Hat and Sword* in the Rockhill Nelson Gallery of Art in Kansas City should be assigned. In this picture, as in the portrait of Laura Battiferri, Agnolo appears to return to an enfeebled version of Pontormo's style in the face of the sensitive and dreamy youth with his hands resting on the chased hilt of the sword, which looks more like the ornament of a gentleman than a weapon capable of inflicting mortal wounds.

Among the many friends that Bronzino had over the course of his life, one of the closest was Luca Martini (Florence ?–1561), a notary and Dante scholar of some merit to whom many of the painter's sonnets were addressed. In 1541 he was made Administrator of the Accademia degli Umidi, later the Accademia Fiorentina. A friend of Varchi's, of Annibal Caro's, and of the most important Florentine men of letters and artists, from Cellini to Tribolo and from Tasso to Pierino from Vinci, he had served the duke in a variety of posts: in 1546 he was Administrator for the construction of the Loggia of the Mercato Nuovo, to a design by Tasso, and, a year later, appointed "Ducal Administrator of the Office of Channels and Galleys," with responsibility for the organization of drainage work in the Pisan marshes.

It was the very malaria that he had been given the task of combating that struck him down, leaving a gap that could not be filled among his friends, who, like Bronzino, lamented his death in numerous sonnets, as was the custom in those days.

Agnolo had portrayed him, presumably during his first stay in Pisa in 1550-1, "in a very beautiful picture of Our Lady, [...] with a basket of fruit, for his having been minister and administrator for the said Lord Duke in the draining of the marshes and other waters, which kept the country around Pisa unhealthy, and consequently for having made it fertile and abundant in yield [...]" (Vasari). Although this painting has now been lost, a record of it survives in a painting by Bronzino's workshop in the Pinacoteca of Faenza, in which the figure of Luca appears by itself, with a basket of fruit. The *Portrait of Luca Martini* in the Galleria Palatina, in which he is carrying a plan of the Pisan marshes, alluding to the work he had carried out, also appears to derive from the painting mentioned by Vasari. Usually dated to the fifties, the picture should actually be assigned to a later time than has been thought up to now, to judge by the advanced style of the painting, suggesting that it was executed in the sixties, either just before the death of the subject or shortly after it, in which case it would be, and this is a quite credible hypothesis, a posthumous and commemorative portrait.

Bronzino also had to thank Martini for as important a commission as the one he received, in 1554, from Bartolommeo Forcoli, a member of the Board of Trustees of Pisa Cathedral, for the altarpiece of the Graces, "in which he depicted Christ naked with the cross, and around him many saints, including a flayed St Bartholomew, which appears to be the real anatomy of a man who has actually been flayed, so natural it is and so accurately copied from an anatomy [...]" Vasari. Two pieces of this panel, which was finished in 1556, removed as early as 1588 owing to its poor state of preservation, and wrongly thought to have been lost by scholars, can be seen in the collections of the Accademia di San Luca in Rome. Of the six original saints,

these depict *Saint Andrew*, kneeling and with his gaze turned upward and to the left, presumably in the direction of Christ bearing the cross, and *Saint Bartholomew*, an image of which Vasari expressed great admiration and which was located to the right on the other side, displaying his flayed limbs like a cadaver on a table during an anatomy lesson.

Another notary who was a friend of Bronzino's and enjoyed Vasari's confidence was the Pistoian Ser Carlo di Michele Gherardi (Pistoia 1505-Florence 1581), for whom the artist "did several paintings [including], in addition to the portrait of Ser Carlo himself, a beautiful Judith placing the head of Holophernes in a basket: on the cover of this picture, for use as a mirror, he did a Prudence gazing at her reflection. For the same man he painted a picture of Our Lady that is one of the finest things he has ever done, for its design and relief are extraordinary" (Vasari). While the latter is now unani-

mously identified with the *Stroganoff Holy Family* (Moscow, Pushkin Museum), although it is not clear on what grounds, it appears to me that the *Prudence* on the cover must be the same as the panel painted with a nude girl seated on a globe and looking at herself in the mirror, set in a rich original frame, perhaps carved by Domenico di Tasso, in the Casa Vasari in Arezzo. The picture is in the style of Bronzino's late work, as exemplified by the *Allegory of Happiness* in the Uffizi, dating from 1567.

His output of mainly religious paintings in the closing years of his life includes one of the most successful of the painter's late works, the *Noli me tangere* now in the Louvre and originally in the Cavalcanti Chapel in Santo Spirito. Finished in 1561 after a lapse of several years, the altarpiece seems to hark back to the refinements of Eleonora's chapel, especially in the ivory-white figure of Christ, portrayed in an elegant pose while

73. *Allegory of Prudence*
35x24 cm
Arezzo, Casa Vasari

74. *Stroganoff Holy Family*
117x99 cm
Moscow, Pushkin Museum

75, 76. Noli me tangere
291x195 cm
Paris, Louvre

Mary Magdalene approaches. In the background are set some splendid still lifes and a limpid and distinct landscape in greenish-blue tones. But the elderly artist's greatest efforts were concentrated on the two large altarpieces commissioned from him by Cosimo I, one for Santo Stefano dei Cavalieri in Pisa (where it can still be seen today) depicting the *Nativity* and another of the *Deposition* (Florence, Galleria dell'Accademia) for the Observant Monastery in Cosmopoli (now Portoferraio) on the island of Elba. They were completed at the beginning and end of 1565 respectively. Bronzino had begun work on the second one as far back as 1560, setting up his studio in the Libreria di San Lorenzo. He was supplied with a work table by the carpenter Bastiano di Confetto, who was paid in March-April of that year for "several pieces used to make a table for the painter bronzino to paint on to be sent to elba" (ASF, Fabbriche Medicee 21, fols. 70v., 81r.). The long period of gestation, nothing new and explainable by the painter's normal working practice (Borghini, during the work on the temporary decorations of 1565, wrote to Vasari on September 21 of that year that "Bronzino is going slowly, as usual"), may have been extended by his advanced age, which forced him to take even longer and to rely increasingly on his assistants in the workshop, in particular his favorite and artistic heir Alessandro Allori. Although the poor state of preservation of the *Deposition*, delivered along with the *Nativity* in Pisa on February 11, 1565, makes a fair judgment impossible, signs of Agnolo's progressive decline have been recognized in it. And it is true that the over-complicated composition, with its exaggerated pathos and the desperation of the figures standing around Christ's body, is a long way from the Olympian assurance of the forties. In the *Nativity* in Pisa, on the contrary, the painter showed that he could still draw on a vein of creativity in the merry crowd of onlookers around the Infant Jesus and in the ring of flying angels, including the one who, in the distance and bathed in light, is rousing the shepherds from their slumber.

The theme of the *Pietà*, which had a deep resonance for the artist as he made ready to die like a good Christian, in the certainty of the Resurrection, is depicted in the panel in Santa Croce (1565-70), where the composition turns on the Virgin's sorrowful face as she gazes in disbelief at her dead Son, and in the small but precious painting on copper that he executed around 1567 for Prince Francesco or, more likely, his wife Joan of Austria.

The last years of Bronzino's life were marked by respect and admiration from all and by honors and rewards, such as his appointment as Reformer of the Accademia del Disegno in 1561, a position that was confirmed ten years later when the institution managed to break away from the Guild of Doctors and Apothecaries, and followed by the post of the Consulate, which he held from June 15 to August 19, 1572. In the meantime redress had been made for the affront he had suffered in 1547, with his expulsion from the Accademia Fiorentina. He was readmitted to the illustrious assembly on May 26, 1566, on the basis of the *Tre canzoni sorelle* he had written and dedicated to Duke Cosimo.

Although the fresco of the *Martyrdom of St Lawrence* in the church of San Lorenzo, unveiled to the public on the saint's feast day, August 10, 1569, was not the artist's last work (afterward he painted the *Raising of Jairus's Daughter* in Santa Maria Novella and

77. Pietà
42x30 cm
Florence, Uffizi

78. Pietà
210x85 cm
Florence, Santa Croce

the unfinished *Immaculate Conception* in the church of the Regina della Pace), it does constitute Bronzino's artistic testament. In it he portrayed himself, on the left beneath a statue of Mercury, the protector of artists, along with his beloved master Pontormo, who had died twelve years previously, and another artist, perhaps his favorite pupil Alessandro Allori, thirty-four years old at the time. While the composition has a disjointed and artificial appearance, thronged as it is with naked figures in affected poses in the manner of Michelangelo, with strained foreshortenings and Mannerist twistings against a backdrop of classical architecture, it is in the surviving drawings – including one in the Louvre (no. 10900) of the figure seen from the back on the far left, attributed

79. Deposition of Christ
350x235 cm
Florence, Galleria
dell'Accademia

80, 81. Martyrdom of Saint
Lawrance and detail, portraits
of Bronzino, Pontormo, and
Alessandro Allori
Florence, San Lorenzo

to the artist by Smyth, and another in the Uffizi (no. 10220 F) of the young man blowing on the coals of the gridiron – that it is still possible to recognize the gifts of the now elderly painter, to the last a great draftsman capable of representing anatomy accurately and with a steady and sure hand.

In November 1572 Bronzino, who had made his will on January 18, 1561, leaving his possessions to his niece Diamante and to the widow and orphans of his friend, the sword-maker Tofano, and all his drawings and instruments to Alessandro, succumbed to the sickness that would eventually lead to his death. Borghini expressed his concern to Vasari in a letter written on the 15th: "Bronzino is ill, and with a sickness of some gravity; yesterday he appeared a little better, and we shall see, for he is old and God help him." In another letter on the 22nd he had given up hope that the elderly artist might recover, and in fact it was on the following day, Sunday November 23, that he passed away, in the house of the Allori where he had lived for most of his life. "At his funeral," Borghini again records, "no one from the world of art, whether painter

or sculptor, was missing, not even Michel di Ridolfo, who dragged his legs behind him." The service that ended with the artist's burial in the church of San Cristoforo degli Adimari, close to the Cathedral, and was attended by the members of the Accademia del Disegno, was not the solemn funeral that Vasari would have wished, but it was certainly in line with the desires of Bronzino himself, averse to pomp and ceremony. A few years before his death, the artist and biographer from Arezzo had described him as follows: "Bronzino has been and is a very kind and gracious friend. He has been generous and loving with his possessions, as much as possible for a noble artist such as he. He has a peaceable nature, and has never done harm to anyone, and has always been fond of all the able men of his profession."

His artistic career and life is admirably summed up in the epitaph composed for his tomb, now vanished, by his devoted disciple Alessandro Allori: "He does not die who lives as Bronzin lived: / His soul is in heaven, his bones are here, his name on earth / is renowned, wherever he sung, painted, and wrote."

Bibliography

A. FURNO, *La vita e le rime di Angiolo Bronzino*, Pistoia 1902.

A. Mc COMB, *Agnolo Bronzino. His Life and Works*, Cambridge (Mass.) 1928.

C.H. SMYTH, "The Earliest Works of Bronzino," in *The Art Bulletin*, XXXI, September 1949, pp. 184-210.

A. EMILIANI, *Il Bronzino*, Busto Arsizio 1960.

J. COX-REARICK, "Some Early Drawings by Bronzino," in *Master Drawings*, II, no. 4, 1964, pp. 363-82.

C.H. SMYTH, *Bronzino as Draughtsman. An Introduction*, New York 1971.

E. BACCHESCHI, *L'opera completa di Bronzino*, Milan 1973.

A. ALLEGRI and A. CECCHI, *Palazzo Vecchio e i Medici*, Florence 1980.

C. Mc CORQUODALE, *Bronzino*, London 1981.

J. COX-REARICK, "Two Studies for Bronzino's Lost Noli me tangere," in *Master Drawings*, 1981, pp. 289-93.

J. COX-REARICK, "Bronzino's Young Woman with Her Little Boy," in *Studies in the History of Art*, National Gallery of Art, Washington 1982, pp. 67-79.

R.B. SIMON, "Bronzino's Portrait of Cosimo I in Armour," in *The Burlington Magazine*, CXXV, 1983, pp. 527-39.

E. CROPPER, "Prolegomena to a New Interpretation of Bronzino's Florentine Portraits," in *Renaissance Studies in Honor of Craig Hugh Smyth*, Florence 1985, II, pp. 149-60.

A. CECCHI, "La Prudenza del Bronzino per Ser Carlo Gherardi," in *Antichità Viva*, XXVI, no. 3, 1987, pp. 19-22.

J. COX-REARICK, "A St Sebastian by Bronzino," in *The Burlington Magazine*, CXXIX, 1008, 1987, pp. 155-62.

A. BRONZINO, *Rime in burla*, edited by F. Petrucci Nardelli, Rome 1988.

A. CECCHI, "'Famose Frondi de cui santi honori...'; un sonetto del Varchi e il ritratto di Lorenzo Lenzi dipinto dal Bronzino," in *Artista*, 1990, pp. 8-19.

A. CECCHI, "Il Bronzino, Benedetto Varchi e l'Accademia Fiorentina: ritratti di poeti, letterati e personaggi illustri della corte medicea," in *Antichità Viva*, XXX, nos. 1-2, 1991, pp. 17-28.

J. COX-REARICK, "Deux Dessins de Bronzino (1503-1572) découverts au Louvre," in *Revue du Louvre et des Musées de France*, 5-6, 1991, pp. 35-47.

E. PILLIOD, "Bronzino's Household," in *The Burlington Magazine*, CXXXIV, 1991, pp. 92-100.

E. PILLIOD, "Le Noli me tangere de Bronzino (1503-1572) et la décoration de la Chapelle Cavalcanti de l'Eglise Santo Spirito à Florence," in *Revue du Louvre et des Musées de France*, nos. 5-6, 1991, pp. 50-61.

L. MENDELSOHN, "L'Allegoria di Londra del Bronzino e la retorica di carnevale," in *Kunst des Cinquecento in der Toskana*, Italienische Forschungen, herausgegeben vom Kunsthistorischen Institut in Florenz, Dritte Folge, Band XVII, München, 1992, pp. 152-167.

J. NELSON, "Dante's Portraits in Sixteenth Century Florence," in *Gazette des Beaux Arts*, 6, ser. CXIX, 1992, pp. 59-77.

J. COX-REARICK, *Bronzino's Chapel of Eleonora in the Palazzo Vecchio*, Berkeley-Los Angeles-Oxford 1993.

J. NELSON, "Agnolo Bronzino's Portraits of Luca Martini," in course of publication in *Mitteilungen des Kunsthistorischen Institut in Florenz*.

L. WALDMANN, "Bronzino's Cambi Altarpiece for Santa Trinita," in course of publication in *Mitteilungen des Kunsthistorischen Institut in Florenz*.

Index of Illustrations

THE GREAT MASTERS OF ART

Andrea del Sarto
Benozzo Gozzoli
Bernini
Botticelli
Brunelleschi
Canaletto
Caravaggio
Carpaccio
Cellini
Cimabue
Correggio
Della Robbia
Domenico Ghirlandaio

Donatello
Duccio
Filippo Lippi
Fra Angelico
Giotto
Giovanni Bellini
Leonardo da Vinci
Luca Signorelli
Mantegna
Masaccio
Michelangelo
Piero della Francesca
Pietro and Ambrogio Lorenzetti

Pontormo / Rosso Fiorentino
Paolo Uccello / Domenico Veneziano / Andrea del Castagno
Raphael
Simone Martini
Titian

Forthcoming monographs:

Tiepolo
Perugino